MY FATHER'S SHADOW

MY FATHER'S
SHADOW

Constance B. Teele

To order additional copies of this book, contact:
Xlibris Corporation
1-888-795-4274
www.Xlibris.com
Orders@Xlibris.com
19851

CONTENTS

V RELIGION

VI IDEAS/OPINIONS

VII CANCER

VIII DAD

INTRODUCTION

This book is dedicated to my Father, Shirley A. Beasley Jr. Dad was a true Poet. My Dad's excerpts you will be able to read in a special section of this book. Thanks Mom for allowing me to publish Dad's great work.

My intentions were not only to present you with poetry, but real life thoughts and feelings. In doing so, I speak a lot about different aspects of life with a finale at the end of a fictional story, based on the war of drugs. Go with me on a journey of life with great and broken promises, heartaches and pain, endurance and struggles and the two most important things, God and Love.

God has always been part of my life. It took me almost forty years to put him first. If I only knew then what I was missing, I would have done it a long time ago. The possibilities now are endless and my blessings have been countless.

SPECIAL THANKS

To the late Rev. John Price
Sylvia and Luther Woods
Maceo Dickason
Louise Brown (Annie Lester)
To Mrs. Mary Warren who not only pushed me to get on the ball but took an extra step in bringing me the work of her friend and sending me a check in the mail to help me along the way.
To my copy-editing team:
Dorothy Beasley (Mom)
Anthony Teele (Husband)
Eric Beasley (son)
Darlene Beasley-White (sister)
Rhonda Allen (sister)
Larry Ingram (cousin)
Thanks to all of you for letting me share the works of both Dad and me. Some are writings that I have shared with some of you or wrote for you along the years. Thank you. May God blessings be with you always?

BIOGRAPHY

Hi, my name is Constance Beasley Teele of Christiansburg, Virginia (people call me Connie). I added my maiden name because a lot of people know me by Connie Beasley, and a lot of my poetry was written before 1996 (the year I was married). I am married to an incredibly handsome, God-Loving man named Anthony (Tony) Teele. He is also the person who created the graphics for the cover. I have two grown sons, Andra Sergio and Eric Steven Beasley and one Grandson, Christopher Xavier (Andra's son). I am from a family of eight, three sisters and two brothers, and two stepbrothers, which I have yet to meet. Freda, the oldest, wants to put us all in a toothpaste commercial. Is there someone out there that would like to check out our smiles?

I presently hold the position of Area Manager at Alliant Techsystems in Radford, Virginia.

I like many of you, beat the odds by having great children as a single parent. Every year some television program has a show about a child who has gone in the wrong direction and they use the single parent household as part of the reason. A lot of successful single parents exist. Can I see the positive side sometimes? It is not whether they have just one parent it's about not leaving God out and giving love, time and attention. That has no price. Even then life is an unpredictable avenue. Unpredictable for all, the poor, the single, two parents, one parent and even the rich.

My work can be found in Sparrowgrass Poetry, International Society of Poets, J. Mark Press, American Poetry Guild and Horizon Poetry Press. On the side I make greeting cards with poetry created uniquely for each individual. Included in this book for your reading pleasure are the works of the late Shirley A. Beasley Jr. (my father). Thanks Mom for sharing and allowing his work to shine

The series you are about to encounter is for the young, the old, the ones that will never be old and even for those that are caught somewhere in between. Come on in, maybe you can relate or maybe you just want to feel the emotion(s). Whatever your reasons for picking up this book, thank you and May God bless you. The opinions are my Dad's and mine. I have added, a special e-mail from my son Andra that I wanted to share with you. I respect all thoughts and ideas and I realize they may not be the same as mine. I also love the way everyone's opinions are not the same.

Wouldn't life be boring if that were not true?

I feel very blessed to have this gift from God and my Dad. Will you share with me the miracles and growth that I have endured through my years with and without Jesus Christ as my personal Savior? Take a chance, peek in and see how God has worked and will continue to work in millions of lives. Who knows, there may be a blessing somewhere just calling your name.

All poems without an author listed are mine.

From my son: Andra

As a child I chose to be the best. I had passion, faith, heart and drive, this is what separated me from the rest but being so different is not always so easy. Going against the grain, doesn't exactly give you many friends, many depressing nights and long days face you when the challenge of success lies in front of you it seems as though it is a goal that few want you to reach. Determining your enemies from friends gets harder and harder the closer you get to your destiny. This isn't a poem or a forward, this is my way of saying thank you and letting you know the behind the scenes of my life and how you affected it.

How did you know?
As a child when you wanted to hug me and hold me when I was hurting, that I needed to be left alone to feel the pain so I could be strong for tomorrow and years to come?
How did you know?
While for years I longed for a father, all I needed was a mother who cared?
How did you know?
When I had a great game or race, I did not need another person complimenting me but I needed, someone critiquing me because my potential had not yet been met?
How did you know?
When I felt like the depth of hell was smashing down on me, to give me a hug?
How did you know?
When I felt like I could do no right, to compliment me on my smallest endeavors?

How did you know?
When I felt like a failure and all alone in college to give me a call to
    say you loved me?
How did you know?
When women crushed my heart, to send me a card to show me
    that you cared?
How did you know?
When I contemplated suicide over issues no one to this day knows
    about, too
offer to come down for a visit?
How did you know?
My life was worth keeping, when at times even today I am not so
    sure?
How did you know?
I was worth loving when no one else seems to think so?
How did you know?
How did you know?
How did you know?
I am not sure how you knew but I thank you

I

IT EXPLAINS
IT REMAINS A POEM

A poem can be laughter and joy,
A poem can be about a man or woman or girl or boy.
It can be about me and it can be about you
No matter what it's a feeling that leaves no doubt.
It can make you laugh and it can make you cry
It can talk about living or the day you die,
It needs no explanation or anticipation,
It explains it remains a poem.

Constance Beasley (Teele) (1978)

WHAT I KNOW

I do not know why I'm here,
I do not know why I came.
I know I came in Jesus' name.
No matter what the task, no matter what the challenge will be,
I want the words of Jesus to be my eyes that I may see.
No matter what road I may take, or where my feet will lead,
It will be the word of God in which my heart will feed.
So I ask in Jesus name let me walk the walk and talk
the talk each and every day,
Let me know the way to call on you and guide me as I pray.
Power is through God; all I have to do is ask,
Let me put you first and everything after last.
You are the reason that I am here you died to save my life,
And no matter what my life endures nothing can compare to
your struggle and your strife.
I had no nails put in my hands nor was I hung upon a cross.
I did not die to save a soul or heal those of us that's lost.
I did not fast for forty days nor heal the sick and lame,
I did not let them beat me up love and forgive them
just the same.
I did not hang upon a cross to pay the sinner's fee,
The pain of death that Jesus' endured for all of us to see.
Real pain and suffering the way that only Jesus knows,
All of this just for us so he can save our soul.
Yet God's own-begotten son gave up his life for me.
My God my God from me to you what will your reward be?

II
SINGLE

ARE YOU SINGLE?

You know how you think no one else could be going through the same old-crap that you are? Perhaps you too have gone through life man after man each one different. Yet all of the men seemed to have some dark secret that you will soon discover. Do you call or not call? Do you go ahead and go out by yourself? Would that make you seem desperate? These are situations that you may soon or have already embarked upon. Maybe I can help. I know because I've been there. I didn't get married until I was 39 so girls listen up; I learned the rules the hard way.

In high school everyone seemed to be wild, classes were easy so it was always about the fun you could have. I was a sports fanatic football, basketball, track, boxing, you name it. My Mom and Dad were very strict. Mom created and hosted the only activities we were allowed to go to at night. Dating was reserved for school dances only. My girl friend Alisha would always tell me of her adventures with men and how many she had. I always envied her, yet I was scared to death to be as adventurous as she was. Her stories were always juicy and men seemed to flock around her. The same was not true for me you see I did not have that prefect figure (if you know what I mean). Soon I discovered the reason she had no trouble: Men love the word s-e-x. Especially when you are at the age, when those hormones peak.

I finally got to go to a party without my Mom being there. See, my Mom directed the youth center (the only place we were allowed to go) so she had eyes like a hawk. There he was dark and handsome, and one of the most popular football players the school had and he was walking my way. Mmm, I thought to myself but I was determined to handle myself like a lady. He walked up to me and said hi. This man was a catch and ladies watch out, because if you know he is a catch so does someone else. We would go to this place called the duck pond and kiss a little but we never made out. I felt like I needed a little more experience before I could handle this muscular man. My mind would wander as the cold wind blew in my bedroom window. You see it was not school that had my attention, sports, or being a disciple (which at the time did not exist). It was all about me and what I felt was missing. Boy, did I get it, all the wrong answers and a lot of heartbreak and pain. So I sit at home again, alone with the cold wind blowing against my window. Wishing and holding on to my pillow as if I were holding on to the man of my dreams. The nights seemed long and comfort did not seem to be an option. As I laid and closed my eyes, I thought maybe if I could think of something exciting the night would not be so long. Turning, I noticed the clock flashing 2AM and finally my eyes seemed to relax, fading me into sleep.

As I slept, I started having all sorts of thoughts, wishes and dreams. With thoughts of him holding me tightly never leaving my side. At my beck and call caressing me, but as usual, just when he began to speak the alarm went off, time to get up. I had to force myself to exercise every morning, while thinking of all the winches out there that did nothing and ate everything yet never gained a pound. My Mom always said a winch is a good housekeeper. God help me because a good housekeeper is not what I meant.

Out into the world to explore, although alone, I knew this was something I had to do. I kept telling myself tonight would be special. I bathed and put on my red dress, as the stereo played "put on your red dress baby." When I entered the club, I could feel all eyes on me (this is what made all the workouts worthwhile) and I was showing confidence that I never had before. The club had a nice tone, a jazz band, no blue jeans or tennis shoes allowed. I liked this club besides the music, the men dressed. The men dressed in anything from suits to casual wear.

I made them look up my digits, (or do you call the telephone numbers something else these days?). I had to think that it was their choice to call. They seemed to like to whisper sweet nothings in my ear.

Oh, by the way, if they do call you back beware, 30% or more are married, at least 10% have girlfriends and maybe only 2% are actually there trying to find that perfect someone. The other 58% percent only wanted a "booty call."

So you go home and once again, the cold wind blows through your window. Emptiness once again fills your room. Do not get me wrong you have a great time, but at the end of that so-called "good" night you go home and feel the cold wind of loneliness blowing against your window.

Then one day I found a plaque that reminded me to pray. It tells of complaints, worrying, crying and feeling hurt and says we constantly ask "Why Me?" How often do we just knell down and pray? So I got down on my knees, my loneliness by then had caused the tears to overwhelm me. After I finished praying, my life took an unexpected turn. I had no more tears it was like they instantly disappeared. That heavy weight felt as if someone had removed it while I was on my knees. Wow what a feeling. All from getting on my knees and taking time to pray. My thoughts about finding a man changed. If I went somewhere, it was to relax, not to find a man. Praying became part of my regular routine just like my morning work out.

People start to treat me differently. My idea of the "real man" rose to a whole new level. When the cold wind blew through my window, the comfort of the Lord Jesus Christ warmed my soul and loneliness was no more. It seems Christ brought me the man I was longing for. Then tomorrow became something different, not the same old thing but a new day.

DO YOU FEEL THE HEAT? OR IS THE COLD WINDS BLOWING THROUGH YOUR WINDOW? WARMTH SHOULD FIRST COME FROM GOD NOT MEN.

RETURNED LOVE

What about the one you care about?
Do you show your love?
I would have stayed by your side no matter what
you would say or do,
That's because I love you.
You could have been right or wrong but in the end
I would have gone along.
Do you have feelings for me at all?
Why do you call me the names you call?
You should have been good to the one that loves you,
You'll need me, I'm sure you do,
When there's no one around to talk to, when you're down and
when you're blue.
The perfect person to cheer you up,
And does it with a special touch.
Is the one that love's you.
I will love you until the day you die,
I will laugh with you and even cry.
I will give you space and set you free,
I just want a day together just you and me.
A day of conversation,
I will keep out of your relations.
I will not press my love on,
I will not cry on your shoulder or over the phone.
My tears will remain inside my home
Even though you leave me all alone,
I'll still love you.

Connie Beasley Teele (1976)

THE MAN OF MY DREAMS

When the moon is blue and the weather is cool,
I would love to be with you.
When stars are bright with the gleaming light,
We could share only a lover's delight.
Just to hear you whisper sweet words in my ear,
The thoughts of not being with you, brings my eyes into tears.
Your skin feels as soft as shiny silk,
I love the way your body's built.
I try not to be a fool,
But man I love to be with you.

Connie Beasley (1975)

MISSING YOU

As I go throughout the day and you are not around,
I want to reach out and touch you, but your hand
cannot be found.
When I leave the house, leaving you behind, it seems
like something's missing,
Holding you tight in my arms or maybe just the
two of us kissing.
My thoughts are what I have to carry me through the day,
My thoughts of loving you, help me along the way.
Yet when I return home, I know I will not be alone.
Because you will be with me once again,
My Husband my lover my friend.

Connie B. Teele

LONELY

I'm Lonely and sad each day through.
Looking for someone to talk to.
A laughing face a hand to hold,
Someone to ask how your day goes.
Someone to speak to and they are never cold,
To be together until your day is done.
To be able to go out and not be alone.
To sit and watch the morning sun.
The world is lonely the world is sad,
The world can make some feel awfully bad.
It's full of hurt and full of sorrow,
Sometimes without hope for a good day tomorrow.
I am lonely,
I am sad,
My days have turned out awfully bad.
As soon as I get upon my feet, someone puts me
back into my seat.
Love and hurt it's the name of the game,
They all dump you, just the same.
A week of happiness for a year of sadness,
Is it worth it? All that madness.

Connie Beasley Icole
June 21 1978

BLOOM MY CHILD

The sun has stopped shining and what you see is rain,
Is this for the grass or Jesus crying out in pain?
Watching God's children turn the other way,
The only thing that we can do is to kneel down and pray.
That they may see their way of living and
where it's taken them to,
That they may see the pain it brings to people,
just like me and you.
It takes a flower and pulls its petal's one by one,
And it will not stop until there is none.
That beautiful flower that brought sunshine to someone's life,
The flower has withered away because of a world of
trouble and strife?
Their roots have not yet died so we can work and care for them,
That someday that flower will grow again with
its beauty from limb to limb.
You are my flower and I know your roots are there,
I'm looking forward to seeing them bloom,
because I love you and I care.

THE SINGLE PARENT

I built a world with children with no one else but me
It was too quick the time was short but I must pay the fee.
Sometimes it's full of laughter and good times or within,
It's just like Love and hate, but the line is very thin.
The criticism from others can make you feel really low,
But I will survive, with my brains, instead of someone's
pocket full of doe.
I'm still a woman do you hear me, and yes I'm still proud,
I'm not a silent listener I say my thoughts out loud.
I may have built some lives, in a way that some may not allow,
But when my children are grown they'll say.
That's my Mama and I'm proud.
If you look into the mirror and see your life, remember she chose
life, instead of the choice to kill,
Aren't you glad your mother decided to give birth to you, so
today you may live?
It's so different when the choice is on the other side,
It's so different when you know you could be one that died.
So do not put me down, lift me up and say,
I love you as much as yesterday and even more today.

1980 Connie Beasley (Teele)

SACRIFICE

I met you and it was like the sun rose,
You gave me love and I began to glow.
You vowed to love me until I would die,
I can see being with me now has made your life really hard,
I know deep in my heart, we will never part.
Never will I let you suffer, not even for a day,
My pain will never be your pain to help you I must say.
I'm letting you go my dear,
It's because I care.
For as endure my life in pain,
I will not let you watch or hold my hand
Or feel that you have lived your life in vain.
Please don't try to talk to me,
Or try to change my mind you see.
Because my Love for you is so,
I have to let you go and grow.
Say goodbye and pray for me.
For soon, the good Lord's hand is where I'll be.
I love you with all my heart,
This is the way we must part, for my pain is
mine just let me be.
You will be better off I know you'll see.
Take care and let your life go on,
Take Care and goodbye; is what I'll say?
For tomorrow will be a brand-new day.
I love you

DESTINE TO UNHAPPINESS

I never thought happiness was meant for a person like me,
Then there it was, a flicker of light that only I could see,
A key hung in the air I think it's meant for me.
The key opened the door and then my life began,
A lovely life of happiness I thought would never end.
It started with your voice so kind it showed that you cared
You threw away my past a life I often feared.
You took that fear and threw it out and left no room for doubt.
You gave me your guidance combined with love,
which no one else had done,
You gave me a reason to want life, and proved the
battle can be won.
Today you are so distant but you must know
I learnt a lot from you and now I believe,
Love and caring is somewhere just waiting on me.

III
LOVE

A HALF OF A
LIFETIME OF LOVE

Look at you two like newlyweds after 50 years
You have endured the challenge and made it through the fears.
Fifty years that's half a century you have been together
And today you vow your love once more,
but this time it is forever,
Fifty years ago on Saturday you vowed your love to God,
In sickness and in health, till death, do you part?
You knew no one else could change it, once you said I do,
No one could take away the vows you made to him or
the vows he made to you.
The road was not perfect it had its curves and hills,
It even had a rock or two and of course it had its thrills.
Yet you knew you made those vows together the vow
you made to God above,
And that's the vow that keeps you together the vow
you made of love.
Till death, do you part, in sickness and in health, till death,
do you part in sickness and health.
Think
You held it together while so many others sank.
Trials and tribulations they are in a marriage too,
It's not the trials and tribulations it's what you decide to do.
One Hundred Percent, one had to give when the other
had fallen down,
One Hundred Percent, to pull them up, till their feet touched
solidly on the ground.

Now after 50 years through the laughter and through the tears,
You look into each other's eyes once again,
this time past the fears.
And you say I do again because your love is true,
A vow not only for both of you, but a vow made to God too.
Written for Rev. John Price and
Mrs. Bea Price celebrating 50 years

BROKEN HEART

It hurts like a cut
It takes so long to heal
It drains inner strength and leaves outer weakness
It can change a smile into tears in less than a second
It can change courage to fears
All the changes can happen in the blink of the eye
It changes lifestyles
It changes your means of being
It's just like a clock that some day stops ticking
The pain for caring
A broken heart

1980
Constance Beasley (Teele)

BROKEN VOW

It 's like the razor blade sliced across the veins on both hands,
The blood continues to drop until you can no longer stand.
I cried Lord please help me I don't know what to do,
I know my decision can't be made without me going first to you.
It throbs and it throbs even when I think
it could throb no more,
The pain from inside my heart comes knocking at my door,
Will the pain ever stop? Can love really heal my wound?
If love is the answer, it needs to show up soon.
I'm fading; I'm fading not knowing if I can hold on,
Will it be on time?
Or will I be long gone.
It's taking away my strength and I'm feeling real weak,
I'm trying to stop the bleeding but it seems to have a leak.
The fingers on the left hand are pale and lost their look,
It's just a little chapter inside of life's long book.
Here come the tears again, please, make them go away,
I made a vow to God, now what am I to say?
Please make it go away, I seem to not know how,
To wipe away the tears, or bring about a smile.
Please, make it go away I cannot stand the pain,
The blood is running harder now, through each and every vein.
Let go of the razor blade please . . . take it off my wrist,
Hold me in your arms I need a gentle kiss.

By Constance B. Teele

THE DIETER

Sometimes we feel discouraged and everyone puts us down,
Sometimes we sit and cry when no one is around.
Don't they see we are human too?
How would you feel if someone said mean things to you?
Take me for a walk, hold my hand and be my friend.
Don't push me out, or lead me astray,
Hold my hand and led the way.
Your fussing will hold me back and send me on a binge in fact.
So if you really want to help me out,
Just take me by the hand,
Don't say I can't or think I won't, show me that I can.
We all are God's creations as beautiful as can be,
We can join together, together you and me.
Show your love by giving me your help don't call me names and
such,
Make my change be, because, you've helped me so much.
So if you really love me and you want my strength to grow,
Don't call me names and cut me down I need your love, you
know.
Help me exercise and laugh with me, show me that you care,
Teach me to love my body, take away my fear.
Let's take a walk or play a game and make it fun for me,
In the end we will both be happy and healthy as can be.

IV

TRIBUTES

TO MY DARLING SONS

It's funny being a parent not being at every game,
Although my thoughts and prayers are with you,
I know it's not the same.
I too, would like to watch you make those tackles or
even run the ball,
I too, would like to yell at the coach or
the referees that made the call.
I am so proud of you and all you seem to do,
Just remember after every play Mom really loves you.
And if she could, she would be there today and
everyday rain, sleet, or snow.
My thoughts and prayers are with you no matter what you do,
or where you go.
So be careful, my sons, remember Mom loves you,
And you are Mom's special, NO.2.
For Andra Beasley and Eric Beasley
Love Mom

A MOTHER'S JOY

When you were born I held you rocked you and told you
how you're loved,
I prayed to have angels watch over you to our Savior up above.
I did not know what you would grow up to be,
or how you would turn out,
But I knew my love would be never ending that
I knew without a doubt.
You used to come in crying and I would wipe away your tears,
You used to come in so afraid I would tell you not to fear.
We all taught you how to pray and we asked
God to protect us all,
And when you start to stumble we knew
God would break your fall.
Now that you are grown with tears of joy inside my eyes
God has made you a prophet to help us reach the sky.
Don't think he's just a young boy trying to tell you what to do,
Remember God sent his son Jesus as a young man too.
So as you hear the words of God,
from a young man
Remember, that it's not the age, anyone can be saved, and yes
even you can.

By: Connie Beasley Teele (for Eric Beasley)

A MOTHER

A Mother is a gift from God; her strength is oh so strong,
She carried me and changed her body for me for
nine months long.
Although she could not see me, she loved me every day.
And her strength helped me grow in a very special way.
I even kicked her in the gut and you know what?
She just laughed and rubbed my feet.
Even though I was inside her stomach I knew
my mom was sweet.
Though my birth would take hours she held on
strong and tight,
It was just like Mom to make everything all right.
She fed me and held me with a smile upon her face,
Even at 3a.m.in the morning when I needed her to wake.
When I took my first step she held my hand,
and did not let me fall,
If Mom, could have that kind of strength
I'm bound to conquer all.
Now that I am older you are still right by my side,
Whether it is on this earth or in the big blue sky,
Just as I felt your love for nine months without
being able to see your face,
No matter where I am I can feel your love in
each and every place.
What greater love except for that of God could anyone know?
What greater love than that of a Mom could anyone show?
How many would change their body to create a life for one?
Enduring all kinds of changes until your months are done.

Thank you Mom for allowing me to be a part of you,
Thank you Mom for all the things that I did not see you do.
I love you Mom, and could never doubt the
love you have for me,
Because for my life to begin, Mom, it was you who held the key.

By Constance B. Teele

GRANDMOTHERS

I want to tell you about some people that God has sent to me,
At first they made our parents and all that they could be.
They cried with them laughed with them, prayed for them,
then they didn't stop,
They started pouring out more love not leaving out a drop.
Through everyone's trials and tribulations
you never left our side,
I know you are an angel and God has been your guide.
When others could not take anymore and
they were all tired out,
We knew that we could count on you to be there
without a doubt.
Their strength is so remarkable it is beyond compare,
When no one else was able Grandmother, was always there.
If I had one wish in this world
I know what it would be,
To give you back all the love that you have given me.
I can only hope that it is in us too,
A portion of that Angel that we see in you.
So on this day as we make a vow to
God on our love for each other,
A vow is made from love, the same as the love
shared for Grandmother

Constance B. Teele

Written for William and Amelia Foster in honor of their
grandmother's at their wedding

MY PASTOR AND HIS WIFE

Dedicated to Rev. John Price and Beatrice Price
There are few that have showed the true meaning of love,
There are not many that know how to use
the help of God above.
You both held onto God's unchanging hand and
you've made it through,
When there were so many others that were not able to.
Your road may not have been easy but your love was oh so
strong,
It's carried you through the years and kept you going this long.
For the family, community, and friends
you joined together as one,
Never stopping until your work is done.
The love you have for each other you have shared with all of us,
And for the special feelings our lives indeed are touched.
When you look into each other eyes, I see the sparkle there,
The love you have from the first I do,
I see today from the two of you.
For all the years you have endured pain, tears,
laughter and joy as one,
For your courage, strength, love for each other and
the things that you have done.
It has shown that with Gods help everything will be all right,
And that's why for all those years we honor you tonight
our Pastor and wife.

By: Constance B. Teele

BLACK HISTORY

Not realizing I believe that George Washington Carver's
promise to himself today many of us live by
To the greatest good for the greatest number of people
He gave up higher pay so he could teach blacks Scientific
Farming at Tuskegee Institute,
Jane Pittman, a slave, sure she could have freed herself and let
the others stay,
But she spent her life showing others the way.
Kareem, meaning 'noble', Abdul, meaning 'servant of God' and
Jabbar, meaning 'powerful' could do anything or go anywhere,
Yet he spoke out against racism despite
anyone's remarks or stares.
He is a noble powerful servant of God
Rosa Parks got fired trying to fight for a seat on the bus for all
Yet she did not stop until she changed the law
Did you sit upon a bus this week?
Did you cheer at a basketball game?
Have you been, to a store or a restaurant where
everyone was treated the same?
We can because of all the people in history
I only named a very few,
So, please research because there are others and
it could include you too.
Black history has many accomplishments but
the greatest thing of all,
Black history has helped many stand and
changed many unfair laws.
Just by doing one thing it's really not hard at all.

The greatest good for the greatest number of people so our
accomplishments do not fall.
Think about it as you walk down the streets,
As you sit where you want as you choose where or what to eat.
The greatest good for the greatest number of people
We must continue this.
Because if we don't times will go back, and what will our
children miss?

WHEN IT'S ALL SAID AND DONE

The End of Black History Month
We had a month of learning do we let it stop there,
Have you been listening, what will we do with what we hear?
The speakers try to make us stronger so we can join the fight
The hero's made life easier so we can endure
the struggle and the strife
Let's not take a month and let the year go by
Let's not only teach our children how to walk
let's teach them how to fly
What will we tell our children will there be things that
we have done?
To assure our days do not end up filled with clouds and
they too can feel the sun.
Our freedom still depends on us as we go throughout each day.
Our freedom depends on us what we do and what we say.
Our heroes gave us freedom God has given us strength to
continue the fight,
To be able to say what we can do and assure that
we keep our rights.
What will we do now?

Connie Beasley Teele

MS. ANNIE LESTER

This poem is about a lady that went to our church she would always have the Holy Spirit. Matter of fact, at that time she seemed to be the only one that would shout. She would stand and give her testimony; I always thought it was neat. I used to say to myself, that's what I want to be able to do. I want to be able to shout like her, one day. Others would look with their nose in the air. Although I was young, I still remember the looks of disapproval some would give. I learn to really like and respect Ms. Annie. She did and said what she believed regardless of the thoughts of others. It was years and Ms. Annie still shouted; why is that special to me, you might ask? At almost 100 years old she gave a man a job, working in the yard, he was new in town just joined the church she just wanted to help. The man ended Ms. Annie's life. For a long time it bothered me. A person that loved the Lord and helped others, gone. Why or how would such an awful thing happen to a wonderful lady? I wrongfully blamed people in the church, for mocking her when she was a true soldier for the Lord. I thought maybe God said that's enough, but why such a terrible way to die. I only found comfort in someone telling me she did not feel it. They truly believed that God took her soul and only her body went through that horrible tragedy. I too now have that belief. I debated whether to put this poem in my book but it haunted me each day until I felt it belonged. I made a lot of people upset with this poem but sometimes we need to look inside ourselves and that includes me. Life presents dangers because of sin. It's not how much we actually go through if we just allowed God to enter in.

Mrs. Annie

I feel her soul was taken to spare her from her pain,
Our souls are protected if we just decide to live life,
somewhat the same.
You never know when or how we may leave this earth,
But God has protected our soul by his own son's birth.
All we have to do is to put Christ in our life,
And God will take you through the trouble and the strife.
Ms. Annie spoke the words from our Savior up above
LOOK INSIDE MY FRIENDS YOU WILL BE SURPRISED
AT WHAT YOU FIND
When all of a sudden you speak to someone because
you care so much.
You hope they understand and not start a fuss
Would others encourage you to go ahead and speak your mind?,
Even if others, don't like, what is said, understanding,
you will find.
LOOK INSIDE MY FRIENDS YOU WILL BE SURPRISED
AT WHAT YOU FIND
When you take away the communication of the people and
what they say,
You raped them from their individuality,
that's what we do today.
I thank you Ms. Lester for all you stood for, and the things that
you would say,
For worshiping our Lord in your own special way.
For standing up against all obstacles for Jesus Christ the Lord,
For being all and all gaining the key to heaven's door.
For teaching others to stand up for Christ today,
For showing us there is no better way.
So for you Ms. Annie as I stand today,
It's to salute your love and joy because there is no better way.
So if you're one that turned up your nose when God's child
stands up and shouts,

Go back and read your bible, because somehow
you're missing out.
And if you still think you are right.
LOOK INSIDE MY FRIEND YOU WILL BE SURPRISED
AT WHAT YOU'LL FIND

THE SPECIAL ONE

God made her special, she was the Mother of her church,
She was like a glow coming from the sun,
when she came upon this earth.
I knew she was an angel I could tell from the smile
upon her face,
And everywhere my Grandmother went; you felt
God's presence in the place.
She could talk to anyone no matter what age they would be,
And to heaven's gates I believe my Grandmother had a key.
God has a place for all of us no matter who we are,
And that place we must find before we go to the heaven
beyond the stars.
She found her place and God was ready for her to leave,
We cried and cried yet none of us grieved.
We knew she was going to a place that she alone had earned,
She had her trials and tribulations and from each of them
she learned.
Maybe I'll be like her and one day it would be,
Up in heaven together my Grandmother and me
She's very special to me,
And special my grandmother will always be.

Connie Beasley (Teele)
Dedicated to Mama Carrie (Carrie Mae Dickason)

GRANDMOTHER MAMA BEA

There was a special someone that whenever you were around,

She would make you laugh and make you cry and
never let you down.

Her smile was like the sun it glowed and shone real bright,

We could visit her in the morning and never leave till night.

We loved the Sunday cooking and the gathering we had there,

Happiness was in the air the way Mama Bea would care.

No one could take that love away the love she gave for free,

No one can steal the memories because of those
she holds the key.

We lost her to our Savior and one day we will be,

In that Magic Kingdom with our Mama Bea.

Dedicated to by Grandmother Beatrice Smith

TO MOM

I wanted to get you an angel because you know that's what you
are,
Only angels have a heart of gold that shines above the stars.
Only angels say kind words even when deep inside they hurt,
Only angels can feel love from beginning to birth.
I am thankful that God had decided to give an angel to me,
And blessed each time another year begins for more of life you'll
see.
You deserve the world but it is not mine to give to you,
So I can only give my prayers and thank God for you too.
Miracles will come for all the love you give and for the things
you do.

Love, your daughter Connie

CHRISTMAS

What is this thing called Christmas?
What is it all about?
On Christmas Eve as you go to bed,
Memories and excitement for the big day ahead.
Gifts are given to express love and to show how thankful we are,
The same as the wise men that traveled so far.
Just like Christmas, anticipation is what they had,
As they climbed up their camels to see this young lad.
But his gift to us cannot be brought you see,
God gave up his begotten son for those like you and me.
Would you give your son as a present for the world today?
Would you give your son's life, if other lives you would save?
Or maybe your daughter's life as the case may be,
Is that a small price or too big a fee?
He wasn't born with money,
Or from people with high ranks,
He was born, in a building of hay, built from wooden planks.
He started getting turned away while in his mother's womb,
Who would believe one day he would rise from the tomb.
He was as ordinary as I and as ordinary as you.
But he came to earth to save us which he knew he must do.
So as you rise up in the morning and run to look under the tree,
Understand the real present came from a manger the babe who
came to die for you and me.
Do not think about riches they will soon be gone,
But go for a present that will stay so very long.
Longer than forever, whatever could it be?

That babe inside the manger, was he the only key?
The key to the mystery of eternity.
It is a priceless gift of joy, but you must make the choice,
Do you hear him calling?
Can you feel his voice?

IN LOVING MEMORY/
JUNE CHAPMAN

In an office on wheels that was right down the street,
Sat a man of great character, and a heart that's hard to beat.
You see he loved the Lord with all his heart, soul and mind,
And he continuously supported the church and for his
neighbors genuinely kind.
Sure, just like George Jefferson he could hold his own,
But if you had him for a friend you were not alone.
All his friends, cousins, and CB buddies that he would talk to,
I'm sure have special stories that they can share with you.
He thought the young in sports were best,
Like Tiger Woods, what's more to say, we all know the rest.
Or Jeff Gordon on the racetrack,
And our local, Billy Hardee Jr., his cousin at Virginia Tech.
You know he had someone special, who could
turn his life around,
Someone to pick him up when he was feeling down.
She was there when he was well,
She was there when he was sick.
And even in the end that's being there through thin and thick.
She did not turn her back she never did let go,
Mrs. Liz Blake that's real friendship that you show.
With names like JJ, June, Iceman and Tub each name had its
own special meaning to someone.
But one name for him had a special meaning,
To him it was one of the greatest names of all to be Godfather to
a little girl named Tia Greene.

To him she brightened his day like the sun coming up
into the clouds,
Or the stars that shine at night which you could see for miles.
Tia, for June, having you for a Godchild was like having his own
little piece of the rainbow.
You never stop shining, smiling or reaching for the gold,
And believe it or not the rainbow is a pot of gold you can hold.
I can remember his laugh, his jokes but most of all his smile,
A smile that will last not only for a moment, but will stick with
you a little while.
There's something he left for all, to share each day,
A smile, a laugh and a friendly note of love, as we travel along
the way.
So remember no matter what you do or say,
The greatest commandment is love and love was JJ's way.

A TOUCH OF THE HEART

How many people in this world touch many hearts and souls,
How many people can bring you up when you are feeling low?
Always saying something that will put a smile upon your face,
Always pleasant memories each time you leave her place.
Love is what it's all about its Love she spreads around
She used to be the one to pick you up when you've
fallen on the ground.
Love is kind, Love is patient, and love understands all,
The love of a friend is like an angel answering a call.
Loving memories will never cease, neither will my love,
And one day we will join again in that kingdom up above.

Connie Beasley Teele

REVEREND JOHN PRICE

Across the beautiful mountains of West Virginia and through
the valleys of Virginia traveled God's shepherd from
place to place,
When you would meet him, his love glowed
across his Godly face.
He traveled, teaching love is not where you're from or
who you are.
But, all shared true love, both near and afar.
I think he must be an angel, after all, can humans
really love so much?
Yet, he told us time and time it's from Christ Jesus touch.
Show that you have learned from me,
Is what Rev. Price would say,
Go out and spread love across the land today.
Many may not understand, what the body may go through,
Rev. Price did not let go of faith and he wouldn't want you to.
Even when he was weak and thought he could go no more,
Christ stepped right in and held open another door.
So if you think you can't go on, look at the life of
Rev. Price and say,
Through the love and grace our Savior Jesus Christ,
I can make a way.
We will never know the reason, the why we may not see,
Remember Christ said; just remember me.
Rev. Price found the pot of Gold at the end of the rainbow and
he left us with the map,
If you want to see him once again the rules are in your lap.
Hold on to God's everlasting arms, reach for the lifetime goal,

The goal is not found on our body, it's found within our soul.
Rev. Price I thank you for the things that you taught to me
To love and put God first and that rainbow I will see.
So as you sit on that pot of gold, Rev. Price please . . .
save a place for me.

DR. MARTIN LUTHER KING JR.

A Nobel peace prize winner, a hero a warrior no battle too small
Like the disciples of Jesus, Martin Luther King Jr.
answered his call.
Not to fight for our rights and just walk away,
But for the rights of all, regardless of what people had to say.
From protest, fair hiring, voter registration, he was arrested and
they bombed his home,
Yet King did not stop because he knew as long as he had Jesus,
he was not alone.
It was Martin Luther who said, "A nation that chose guns over
butter would starve people and kill itself."
Yet the fight goes on, and I guess it will,
until there's no one left.
We honor him a minister, a hero who believed and lived God's
word until the bitter end,
This man had a dream and managed to make some of his
dream's reality every now and then.
This man left dreams that he had fought so hard to come true,
This man died for his dreams would we dare to?
His memory will live on and so will the dream,
Just like Jesus, many believed, many supported, or so it seemed.
I guess we figure why worry, it was only just a dream
Do we put into action the things that he died for,
So for our children we open a brand new door
Will we stand up or will we only say,
Happy Birthday anyway.
Dr. Martin Luther King

By: Constance Beasley Teele

V

RELIGION

WOMEN OF THE WORD

We have the power because of the angels,
We wonder how we have so much energy.
God gave us that energy the Women of the Word,
Our clothes are of modest material.
Our works are known not bragged about,
We glow because we are the Women of the Word.
No, we do not slander, gossip, or hate,
We realize that these things are of Satan fate.
We are the Women of the Word,
Don't worry we will not turn our backs even if you
bring us down,
If you fall, our hands will help you get back on level ground.
We are the Women of the Word,
Whisper, behind your back we will have none of that,
Because we know that God hears all and that's a common fact.
The Women of the Word

THE ASBURY, UNITED METHODIST CHURCH FAMILY OF CHRISTIANSBURG, VIRGINIA

We're looking, for some friends that we can share our blessings.
Maybe just to sit and talk or share a bible lesson.
Would you like to join us, can we help you out?
The Bible set the rules in case there's any doubt.
Can you look into the mirror and forget just what you see?,
Just remember God said, 'just believe in me'.
The Word is sent from God for all of us to share,
To give us rules to live by to show us that he cares.
The women and men of the Word are disciples just for him,
We will show you how to find the Light when
all the bulbs go dim.
So give us a call we're waiting just for you,
God loves you and we love you too.
A unique and wonderful spirit can be within your soul.
It's not about sitting in the pews or paying your dues.
It's about taking care of God's family reaching out to everyone,
Ours and everyone's brothers, sisters, enemies, children, and
their daughters and sons.
The bible tells us we have power because of the angels please
don't let it go to waste,
We can do it because we are the Men and Women of the church
Wonder what you missing?
Just try a little taste
Of the Asbury, Love and the Asbury, faith . . .

GOD'S HOUSE

Enter into the house where all are welcome in Jesus' name,
If you let your hearts be open, you will not leave the same.
We can rejoice that we are joining together in this Holy building
to worship the Lord.
We can rejoice, thanking God that we can worship together on
one accord.
We can rejoice because he has given each one of us so much,
We can rejoice because we can feel his loving touch.
If you just let go and let God take care of you,
Your lives can be made anew.
Reach out and tell someone you care,
Come and share the family atmosphere.
Because it's Love, the only thing that counts
Just dare open your heart and soul and take in what is said,
When you do this, I guarantee you will be fed.
We're here to win the battle, the battle of Love and Grace,
These are among the things needed to see our Savior face to face.

Constance B. Teele

THERE'S A HOMECOMING GOING ON

Homecoming is often spoke of at funerals when
someone has past,
But this is a homecoming to receive the Lord at last.
So you think that you are ready and your work is done,
Remember that it was God who gave his only begotten son.
We are the plants but we will not wither because
our roots are strong.
We shall grow because there's a homecoming going on.
We have to put on the armor of God,
reach out and touch others.
The rich, poor, the sick, the hungry, the children,
fathers and mothers.
So he, who has ears, let them hear,
How to live by God's word.
You have come to celebrate or find your way back home,
And today, I can assure you, you are not alone.
God will lift all of your burdens, open doors because he cares,
He'll take away your worries and dry all your tears.
Just come on in and leave your burdens you are not alone,
And celebrate with us, because in this house there's a
homecoming going on.

By: Constance Beasley Teele

A LITANY OF FAITH/
BY CONNIE TEELE

O Lord, help us to remember that you are with us
no matter what the circumstances.
Let our faith in you set us free
In gaining wisdom
Lord, give us faith
To endure temptation, for the Lords promised crown
Lord, give us Faith
In the words that we speak and the walk that we walk
Lord, give us faith
Like Rahab, Deborah and Mary, let us believe in your words and
take some time to let you speak to us
Lord, give us faith
Lord, we thank you, for faith and grace.
Rejoicing in the glory in good times and in tribulations.
We know that with tribulation we gain, patience,
experience and hope.
So the blood of Christ now saves us.
Let us be content no matter the circumstances. Amen

THANK YOU LORD

Lord you mean the world to me without you
I would not be here,
When I am down and out you showed me how you cared.
You made the flowers and the grass so green,
You made a lot of creations so beautifully seen.
You died for me so I may live,
Just to show love is all you asked me to give.
Thank you Lord for being there no matter what I do or say,
You were there for me yesterday and
you will be there for me today.
I asked that you strengthen me as I travel through the day,
Help me understand the importance of the things I do and say.
Keep inside my mind when you died upon the cross and when
you rose again,
So that I will understand why I will dare not sin.
So that when I leave this world of yours,
and go to your meeting place,
You'll say, "Well done my child" when we meet face to face.
I thank you Lord for each day that I begin,
And in the name of Jesus I pray that one-day I will live the life
you have for us, the life that never ends.

Connie Beasley (Teele) 1998

WHAT ABOUT GOD

Your mother brought you in this world with love,
It would not be so if it was not for the man above.
God gave us eyes so we can see,
It was God that made you and me.
You respect your mother for what she has done,
God made the earth and he made the sun.
He made the grass and the flowers and the trees,
He made the birds and he made the bees.
But what respect does God get?
He's done more for you than anybody has yet.
We can talk to him when we are down and out,
We can call on him when our minds are in doubt.
He'll fill your life with joy,
He'll treat you the same girl or boy.
He'll forgive you when you have done wrong,
And stay with you no matter how long.
When someone does for us we remember well,
We talk about them, and tell all that we can tell.
But God my God about you how many will we tell?
Are we going to heaven or are we going to hell?

July 22,1978
By Constance Teele

VI
IDEAS/OPINIONS

OLE MAN WINTER

The chill is in the air the trees are without leaves,
You wouldn't dare go out without a shirt with sleeves.
You know OLE man winter is here
The electric bill starts to climb,
Inside is where you dine.
And you know OLE man winter is here
The soup is brewing in the kitchen,
You go out wearing gloves or mittens.
Because you know OLE man winter is here
Of course there is some good to the cold,
To keep warm, you cuddle up you know.
Because you know OLE man winter is here
Crisp as a saltine broken in half,
Snowballs made and, thrown, to make you laugh.
Hot chocolate or a drink to warm the toes,
Handkerchiefs and tissues for the nose.
And you know OLE man winter is here
Sleds riding up and down the hills,
Go to work and pay the bills.
Even though OLE man winter is here

By Constance Teele

DEALERS PLEASE . . . STOP

Do you see how many people you are hurting?
Do you see how many have died?
I have a lot of questions help me find the reason why?
So many of our children die as innocent as can be,
A lot of pain and hardship, everyone to pay a fee.
The drugs have killed neighbors, sisters, brothers, and from grief
a lot of parents too,
Yet, who is the pusher that gives those drugs to you?
You say, you don't have to work like a slave so
you decide to sell dope,
Well who do you think is on the end of that long rope?
You got to watch your back no matter what you do,
You lie for them, you steal for them, some, die for them too.
And all this for someone else, don't you see they're using you.
Who ends up in the prison, which one will take the rap?
Who is the one that has to fear that one might bust a cap?
What have they done for you? Why do you play their game?
Surely they are just your masters, or are you just insane?
When you're all strung—out and have no place to go,
Will they let you in their house? I believe the answer's no.
Think about your choices you know the options there
Think about your family you always know they care.
Count on God he'll help to get you past your fears.
Scared to leave, God is stronger than anyone can be.
And if we join together the right ones will pay the fee.
No more going to jail for them,
No more going out on a limb.
No more killing come on Let's take a stand,

So we can live together in our blessed Savior's land.
So think about what you really want to do,
You are hurting ones that love you and hurting yourself too,
Does the dollar bill mean that much, does money make you
great or does money make you bait?
Use your head, Stop, before it's much too late.
You can control how your name reads on that burial slate.

COLD, COLD WAR

The poem you are about to read will send mixed feelings. It is no reflection on our soldiers, I pray for their safety and for the families in which they belong. One of the greatest things is to give or risk your own life to save others. I really truly believe that sometimes God calls us to fight but that with him being our leader. From prayer and consent not because we think it's right. The vast majority of people realize that what we think is right but sometimes our conscience reminds us it's not really so. With this being said this poem is with great feeling. One of my dear friends has a son in this war. God's children trying to do what is right and God knows that. My feelings on the war are from the heart. I question the real reason and whose interest we were really looking out for. The best thing I got out of war was baptism and prayer that brought tears of joy in my eyes. For all I say put on your full armor the armor of God and put your trust in him.

The Cold, Cold War ——

Don't quote God's word unless you know his word,
Don't say his saying just to be heard.
Do you really want to know what he said?
Vengeance is mine said the Lord,
He didn't say the president of any country including ours or even the
nation's Klan.
Vengeance is mine said the Lord,
Many believe in fighting for what is right,
The blood, the grave all for the red blue and white.
God says do what you want but just so you know,
Your actions have consequences, consequences that will show.

Count on me for all things is what he said,
For it will be too late when we are dead.
In everything we do don't leave me out,
That causes wars, rumors of war, trouble and strife.
And know that he is God Not some idol that we may choose,
Or some man, wearing high, priced shoes.
Who, are we fighting for anyway?
Do we really know or is it whatever the President has to say,
Have you done your research do we know what is real.
Do we have the right to go over there and kill?
Are we the avengers for what they tried to do to his Dad?
Does revenge make, us good? Or does revenge make us bad
The sandstorm is no surprise,
Because God said, I will rise.
There is no other God before me is his word,
Let the earth speak to you if you have not heard.
Its not too late we can prevail,
The problems that we have who shall we tell.
Who can win the violent war?
Who has the key to the impossible door?

MY GOD MY GOD WHY HAVE WE FORSAKEN YOU_

NO TIME SPAN

Life is so confusing, we often question why?
Some of us get to live and some of us die.
We never know the reason and we do not understand,
When one of us is chosen to leave off this land
Yet memory is a funny thing when it comes to death,
For once we think of others and forget about ourselves.
We know that they are special and their ways will live forever.
The special way they live their lives others will endeavor.
The flowers they will bloom and die before the year is out,
The green trees will change colors and the leaves will fall about.
Yet our lives we will never know when the day will come,
That God will say its time to go because your work is done.
The reason is unknown the why we never see,
Remember that God said, "Just believe in me"
And pray that God will take each one into his heavenly care,
And hold them tenderly because one day we will be there.

Dedicated to my Cousin: Charles Carter

TIME?

The roads are rough we know too well,
The trials and tribulation will we win or will we fail?
We do not know how much time there will be.
But we do know God is there for you, just like he is for me.
God is love, and love he had, for everyone whether good or bad.
"I got it like that," he would say,
His own little tone and in his own special way.
His smile and love will live forever within our hearts,
And the love we have for him will never ever part.
If you don't know how and you need some help, remember God
is here and he never left.

In memory of Jimmy Burks

BUILDING BLOCKS

I have no right to talk about you I am human too,
When God made me, he made me just like the likes of you.
It's like the Lego's we come with all the building blocks,
It's what we chose to do with them, that decides the
doors that will unlock.
To build something magnificent or to leave the blocks apart,
To stick them on in the corner and say, tomorrow, I'll start.
To stop on the first try or build something better than before,
To pick up all the pieces when they come stumbling to the floor.
Some chose to take the easy road and be content, and its okay,
Some chose to live their life building for a better day.
Some chose to grow, some choose to use a small amount of
what life gives,
No matter how we choose our life, it's what we decide and
how we live.
We all will answer, for the blocks we chose to use,
God gave us the blocks in his word if we just read and
follow the instructions.
When we choose not to read the instructions
watch out for what you see,
It was not your childhood, it's what you chose to be.
The blocks may stand for a while but when they fall,
what will be the fee?
Follow the instructions they're clear as can be,
And your blocks will shine magnificently for
the entire world to see

Will your blocks stand and endure what may come or will they
remain inside its case
Build your blocks with God's instructions today, for tomorrow
may be too late.

Constance Beasley Teele

VII

CANCER

INTRODUCTION TO POEMS ON CANCER

This section is dedicated to all the people dealing with or sharing life's changes from the disease of cancer. First I give honor to God. I hope if you need courage this helps you along the way. Please have a yearly physical and if it runs in your family tell your doctor the life you may save may be your own. I am sharing some awesome faith I have seen by a few people. I am sure you have stories too. May God bless you.

My Minister from Asbury, United Methodist Church, Rev. John Price Jr., I describe him as an awesome servant for God. He had a lot of influence on my life. This man preached the word like I believe none other would be able to duplicate. He would step on your toes and say if he did, well, because he only works for God. When he first got Cancer, he said how could I complain, look at what Jesus Christ endured. As the years went along the cancer would go in remission and return. Some days his hands were like ice when you touched them. On those days he continued to preach. He got up in the pulpit, each time the spirit of the Lord not only provided him remarkable strength but you could feel the power of Jesus Christ, working through him. The sermons seemed to get stronger. He continued to visit the sick although he would have someone drive for him. He delivered the communion to those who were too sick to make it to church. He prepared the sermon and was going to preach in a wheelchair because cancer had no longer allowed his legs to function and he told me quote, "You don't know how bad I felt when I could not come to preach". Awesome notice it was not the pain I have, but how bad I felt when I could not preach. Reverend Price did get to preach his sermon. He taped the sermon he wanted to give on Easter Sunday. So in church in place of Rev. Price there sat a tape recorder. A chill went through my body and the more I looked up and saw this large tape player where my Preacher once stood the more the tears would flow from my eyes. At first his voice sounded weak but as the tape continued his voice got stronger and stronger, you could feel God's presence. The pulpit again seemed to give him strength even inside a box. He finished by inviting all to come to his home. Each family entered into his private bedroom opened to over 50 people. He had a special word for each of us and handed us a candle and he said when you get in trouble light this candle and pray.

Me, I almost did not make it. I was driving down Interstate 64 to Chester, Virginia, to visit my Grandson. About the time I got almost through Charlottesville the cell phone rang it was my sister telling me Rev. Price was doing something special. My first reaction, he's gotten better hasn't he? She said I am afraid not then she told me about the special event I cried, and did not know how to chose. All along the highway I prayed. Most of the time after a long ride my knees will not let me do much. Today was different, Chris (my grandson) and I went several times around the block, and I played ping-pong with my son (Andra) and his friend Kendra and cards that night. I was reading one of Max Lacado's books when we got in a discussion on faith. It was then I decided to leave at 5a.m. to make it home in time for church. My husband did not get to travel with me because he had to work. He had to visit Rev. Price while we were at church. When I entered the bedroom, this vibrant 73-year-old man said I thought you were out of town. I said yeah until I heard you were preaching; miss your sermon, no way. He smiled and said you came back; I don't even want to let your hand go. He said, don't forget how much I love you and Tony and how much God loves you both. And I said I wouldn't. Before leaving he smiled and said once again, you came back. That I will always remember. He had given me years of joy in the teaching of Christ Jesus. He helped realize that in all, count on Jesus and everything will be all right. In our visits, he told me as he sat with no appetite, legs immobile, every day I look around and find something to be thankful for. I recall once after Sunday school he thought he could not preach, yet, thank God, he walked in the church just in time and reached deep inside and did what thus said the Lord. During Rev. Price's missions you may encounter him anywhere from visiting the jail, community projects, in your home or on the street if you did I bet you too felt the spirit. I found out so many things that where so remarkable allow me to share with you, a few.

A group at Virginia Tech, one year, was trying to celebrate Dr. King's birthday when a string of cars arrived at the stadium bearing the words KKK they approached the group saying the celebration was not going to happen. They did not know what to do. Suddenly out of nowhere, stood a man in a trench coat, fear did not seem to know him he said not only are they going to have this celebration but it will also be bigger than ever because, he was going to invite others. When the new President of Radford University was given his position, at its worst condition in the history of the University the board called a meeting, not seeing the turn around fast enough. Again, out of nowhere, a man stood, not only did he speak up for the President but was able to present the board evidence of his work. He had been president of the NAACP and social activities he remained involved in all as long as he could. He won the senior Bowling tournament, and he could make you laugh and put you in check all in the same sentence. He was none other than a child of God. This is just a small amount of what I can say for such a wonderful man of Christ. Reverend John Price.

Darlene Dickason, was a nurse (married to my cousin Maceo) discovered she had cancer while pregnant. Darlene managed to smile as we visited her in the hospital. He knew he had to lean on God's hands and he held on tight. Maceo's days and nights were long and hard. He watched Darlene's cancer moved remarkably fast. The people on his job gave up time off and donated it to him so he could spend time with his family. To those people and their family I want to thank you, you'll be richly blessed. Maceo and Darlene truly joined together as one. Now he is a single parent taking care of two children and he's back to work another example of God's goodness. He found talking about things helped so he would call his cousin and my sister Evangelist Darlene White. He has accepted the challenge of being a single parent and fought hard for that right. Maceo said that he was going to do this with Gods help. Maceo I am proud of you and Uncle Jack (your Dad) would have been to Then the last one I will talk about although there are many others, and certainly not least is Luther Woods. He is a Production Specialist at Alliant Tech. He told me apparently he had to go through having cancer but he was ready for any thing God wanted him to endure. How awesome to be ready for whatever is planned knowing it won't be easy, yet saying I'm ready. So many people are complaining about little things today. I am guilty of it too, I'm to fat, and life's so unfair to me and so forth and so on. Yet these people among many others fighting for their life continue to feel blessed. They still know were to find their comforter. Not losing the faith despite all things that they endured. Through these lives and others, all still know and say God is an awesome God.

    The following poems are a tribute to these and all others. May God bless you? And build his loving arms around you. The road to life is never promised to be easy, it wasn't easy for his son, and it will not be easy for us.

CANCER

I was walking down the stairs you know, a usual kind of day,
Getting out of bed going to work or play.
I felt that tap upon my shoulder there it goes again,
I felt that tap a month ago didn't bother to look back than.
Shall I check it out, turn my head and see?
What is this thing that keeps taping on me
Oh it's that physical again the one I meant to take,
Yeah, Yeah, I know the sermon, before it is too late.
You already called and set a date for me?
Well my schedule is kind of busy; I guess I have to see.
If I get this thing over with will you quit taping on me?
Well Doc, I know its fine I tried to tell them so,
But I couldn't stop the tapping; it started to
bother me you know.
What? I have cancer please do the test again,
I just played basketball; I was the one that caused the win.
So you see I'm healthy and have no time anyhow,
You see the team they need me, not later but right now.
I can't wait you say my days are running thin,
Cancer can't be happening here it's not even in my kin.
Why would it choose me?
I have a life you see.
Besides my great life I'm healthy as can be,
Oh, and don't forget the team they're counting on me.
What do you mean, if I only listen to the tap
I would be cured by now?
But now the cancer has spread and is too far into my cells.
There is that tap again; what do you want this time?
You started this whole thing; you are messing with my mind.

Pray you say well it's too late for that,
My destiny is spoken my fate I have now met.
What have I to lose I may as well knell and pray after all there's a
lot I been wanting to say,
Maybe he will listen God knows my soul needs a
little comfort today.
If I wait another month, my body might be cold.
The tap was right before the Doctor told me so.
Please forgive me Lord; I hope it's not too late,
A heavy rock, lies on my chest as I view the life that s
peaks my fate.
The tears are flowing down my eyes;
I knew just what they meant,
With prayer my fate has changed I now am heaven sent.
I must go I have a lot of work to do,
So watch out behind you it just might be me, tapping on you.

Constance B. Teele

The story of Michak, Shadrack, Abed-Nego talks of three men who were challenged by the King to give up God or die in the fiery furnace. All their clothes were torn and burned, but their trousers, which were used, to tie them up. The king asked, 'Give up your God or die'. The furnace was heated seven times its normal temperature. When someone goes through the unimaginable, I think of this story. How many, would have given up God. Would they think they were saving their life by giving up, God? Another, is the story of Elijah's in Kings the 19th Chapter of the bible when he thought he couldn't take anymore, so he asked for his life to be taken and the angel said get up and eat, he did but laid back down. Once again the angel said get up and eat. Strengthen by the food he went forty days and forty nights. We too are Strengthen by food. The bread that we partake when taking of the Lord's Supper. The angel is tapping us on the shoulder and asking us to come. Will you come during the storm; will you remain after the storm is over? The pain that some endure may feel like they are inside a furnace. Well, God is right there with you instead of one there are two. Hold on, I know it's hard but most of all after the storm is over. Remember where forth cometh thou help.

Just like the three in Numbers pain has tied me up
with my own,

Promises to let me go if I just give up God alone.

The furnace oh so hot the fire has reach it highest ground,

It's taken my hair; my looks and my body are oh so weak,

Give him up they say or I will take you to your peak.

If he were your God he would have saved you from this pain,

Surely, even you can see holding on to God you have not gained.

I will not listen to the voice or the things it has to say,

For it is God right beside me holding up my head?

You must have thought of me as God's servant to
present me with this test,

You must have thought of me as weak when you took away my
strength and rest.

But I don't live for the body you see it's just a shell,

God has a place for me in his kingdom and I'm not
giving in to your Hell.

So do what you want my reward is yet to come,

You see, my life belongs to God and God will say it's done.

I will lift him up and if you look at me and see two,

Its just God, waiting to endure what is next from you and me.

And when this war is over you will see that we have won.

All will know, I did not walk alone,

God was carrying me than and God will take me home.

So after the storm is over I want you all to know,

The storm never made me weak it only made me grow.

God held me tight and never let me go

So if you going through something and the devil happen to
think he might win,

Know if he had won the battle he wouldn't be
messing with you then

He's trying to win you over because he's losing ground,

Don't give in, God's has got your back and
you are heaven bound.

By Connie Teele

ENDURING/CANCER

Faith as big as arms held wide,
Everything was happening not a single dream set aside.
And than the world came crashing down,
Health has taken you to the ground.
You almost forgot God is there but God held on tight,
He let you know that he loves you with all his might.
Faith as small as a mustard seed he said would make you strong,
Just a little seed could help you go on.
Thank you Lord for now I stand,
Holding tight to an unchanging hand.
I will succeed I will not fail, my life I will not doubt,
Its Christ that brought be through this far and Christ will bring
me out.
So do not shed a tear oh love because I'm saved by grace,
What better way to live your life but knowing, you have reserved
your place.

CHOICES

There is more to life than joy and fun
We will be here until our work is done.
There is more to life than alcohol and drugs.
How about thinking about what it does.
Drown your sorrows for a while,
But afterward they increase a mile.
Sounds like you maybe so,
Or maybe it's someone you know.
It does not make you happy for a short time you forget.
Sometimes you can wake the next morning with a
life full of regret
Happiness is not found in a glass
Or about getting to that lane that is fast.
It's the choice you make and what you do'
Your life of happiness is up to you.
What will your choice be, going through glasses and bottles
checking out what you may find
Or making a change that will ease your mind
If you need an answer Jesus said just ask
And you'll receive true happiness, happiness that will last.

Connie Beasley Teele (1976 and 2002)

DARLENE'S CANCER

Many turn over into their beds when sickness has set in.
But Darlene got up and went to church until the very end
Many lose faith not understanding when someone has to die,
Yet Darlene said to Maceo, "It would be all right
there is no need to cry."
Her faith was strong even in sickness or health although
she did not understand,
She knew what she needed to do is hold on to
God's unchanging hand.
The faith to help her enter into God's paradise,
No more pain and sorrow, but ever lasting life.
So although life brings us situations that we seldom understand,
Holding on to Gods unchanging hand is
something life demands.
Be like Job and hold on with all your might.
And even in despair he will see you through,
Just keep the faith no matter what you do.
You may have questions you may not understand
the reason why,
Trust God he will guide you by and by.

In loving memory of Darlene Dickason

UNCLE BOOTY

James Beasley most called him "Booty".
He was a magician and all of us ran to him
wanting to see a new trick.
He could pluck you so hard it would knock you out,
He didn't lift weights, he worked construction and he was
muscular and strong.
If you visited our town and said his name you can get a story.
Uncle Booty died of throat cancer,
Little children ran up to him each and every day,
Our day seemed not until Uncle Booty showed up to play.
He would put a coin behind his ear, or in the other hand, and it
would disappear and be found in another place;
Nobody could do magic like Uncle Booty could,
I mean nobody can,
As we grew older and watched people around this man
That's when I realized his magic was not only in his hand.
It brought joy that showed on others inside and out.
Like the sun when it shines in the day you knew it was
out and about
Now God promises that we would bear no more than
we could stand,
He's taken away our Uncle into heaven's magical land
Like the birds and the bees and flowers they never really die
The seed remains and the sound lives forever and
will remain by and by.

By Connie Beasley (Teele)

VIII

DAD

DAD

For if we believe that Jesus rose, from the dead, so even then,
those, which sleep in Jesus, will God bring with him.

Shirley, June and Shay slept in Jesus, so there is no doubt God has
taken him home.

Don't you worry family God is here we are not alone.

Remember, there shall be no more pain,

Our Dad is at rest.

Just remember our Father in Heaven; he is the one that knows best.

If only each one of us could see the world like this man,

The question could then be asked, "Can you die tomorrow? Your
answer would be 'Yes I can'.

He fought so we could have sidewalks and sports to name a few,

Not just for his children but for each of you too.

Oh yes, he spoke his mind, and let you know if you were wrong,

But he wouldn't talk about you behind your back or after you
were gone.

Before he went into the operating room, he did not pray for himself.

He prayed for many of you, God's children who are left.

He fought his fight and he has won, his work is finally done,

But for many, our work has just begun.

For us our bond is individual but our love is such as one.

Wife, Sisters, Daughters, kin, friends and of course his special sons.

His firmness and love made us what we are today; no one can tear us
apart,

Because what you gave to us, Dad, you gave us from your heart.

So thanks Dad for being that little piece of leather well put together.

This is not goodbye Dad; we'll see you later on,

When we all meet together in our heavenly fathers home.

Love, Your Daughter Connie

Before I introduce, the works of my belated father Rev. Shirley A. Beasley Jr. I would like to take a little time to give you some background. You see my father was at work one day and he lost his eyesight. He was a real man they would call him, he needed no one, counted on no one. I wanted to write his story but unfortunately it came to an abrupt end when he no longer wanted to talk or answer questions. This information, many of his family and mine will be reading and gaining this knowledge for the first time. Ironically at the same time of his interview I found out my father was raised in the same house I am in today. If you were born in the late fifties or sixties, maybe you can relate. If you were born in the later year's maybe, you too can finally understand why they constantly say, "in my day". Shirley A. Beasley Jr. tells the rest of what is written.

I used to get around and go when I got ready and return when I got ready. I never really noticed the sunset, sunrise or the beauty of the winter and the spring. I particularly like the feel of the fall season, it was cool not hot and I did notice the beauty of the trees. My childhood was so-so. The goodness of children lies within my grandmother and then she passed away. She raised me until I was five or six. My brother used to wear my clothes and my mother would call me, "Shirley Beasley looking, something." That was my father's name also, he left me at the age of seven or so. My stepfather would do anything in the world for me. He treated mom well and built us a house so we could finally move out of Mrs. Kathleen's house. Mrs. Kathleen treated us good even after we left.

When mom was at work I stayed with Aunt Minnie, played Jack's Rocks, hide and seek, and other games, which names I have forgotten. When mom was home, she played with us too, including 'ball'. The ball was rubber and the bat was an old broomstick. We had a dog-named Fildo. Fildo loved for me to take him on long wagon rides.

I wish I could recall my fondest memory as a child, I can't recall but I do remember the worst. When I visited my brother and sister and my brother cut me with a knife saying I wasn't his brother. My sisters and brothers called me names a lot. I preferred to stay with my grandparents. I continued to stay even after my grandmother died but my stepmother was mean. She sold my goat and wouldn't get me a Christmas tree. In my stocking all I got was an orange.

I started working at age eleven and worked until I joined the service at age sixteen. I lied about my age because I felt it was time to leave and this was a way out. My fondest memory in the service was 1948 my son was born in Germany. Then when we left we were not allowed to stay married when we returned to the states. One of my worst memories of the service was when the officer drove me around and would not take me back until my curfew was up and then threw me in the stockade for violating curfew.

I returned back to the states in 1953 that's when I met 'Dot'; I thought she was the prettiest thing I'd ever seen. Her looks would make any man's head turn and her legs were perfect. I stayed, on my own, and dated Dot. I roomed at Autrey Johnson's house in a basement apartment on Harless Street. Life was good. I loved Dot, even though she was 16 and I was 24. So we had to go to North Carolina and get married. I liked being married. After my last child I felt dizzy one day and found out I was a diabetic. I did a lot of dancing when I was young. I would help the police break up fights and take people home. Fights were popular; I broke up plenty and was in quite a few. The fights were something I do not want to talk about because of some of the people involved. But I will tell you this I think about them often. I liked my life and I have no regrets. The house was never empty, the guys would come over we would play cards and drink. I have 8 children, including two in Germany.

My father fell asleep after saying this much. The next day I was hoping for more but he was too tired to talk anymore. My father was once healthy and had a house full of friends. When my father lost his sight, you could go by the house and swear he could see because he would be outside washing the pink Cadillac he once drove. Several years later his kidneys failed and he ended up on dialysis this proceeded with him losing one leg, then the other. Through all that my father found God or maybe he didn't find God because you see even drunk he could recite Bible verses. I believe God was always there saying hey, you hear me, you see me, you know the word. I am here for you. But through all the so-called friends being so loud, made it hard for Dad to hear him. Suddenly the loads of friends reduced to, 'very few friends,' who remained loyal although the cards and alcohol had ceased. Finally Dad could hear God calling his name. It doesn't matter if the story you would tell is different and it does not matter if you do not believe me. All that really matters is that in the end Dad knew when God said, "I will be with you always" he meant, "I will be with you always even till the end of time."

MY FATHER'S OBITUARY

R‌ev. Shirley Amos Beasley, Jr., born in Christiansburg, VA January 3, 1930 departed from this life on Monday, January 22, 2001 at Montgomery Regional Hospital. He was preceded in death by his mother, Beatrice Smith, father, Shirley Beasley, Sr., stepfather, Edward "Rabbit" Smith, and brother, James "Booty" Beasley. Rev. Beasley was survived by his two sisters, Mary Elizabeth Mills, wife of Aubrey Mills, and Ada Mae Bratcher; dearly beloved wife Dorothy Dickason Beasley; six children, Freda Johnson, wife of Alan Johnson, Andra Beasley, Connie Teele, husband of Anthony Teele, Darlene Beasley-White, Ricky Beasley, Rhonda Allen, wife of Erwin Allen; grandchildren, Andra & Eric Beasley, Casey & Alan "A.J." Johnson II, Irvin White II & Nakecia English, David McCall, Maurice Beasley & Erin Janae Allen, Ricky II, Ryan, & Ross Beasley, as well as two sisters-in-law, Beatrice Morgan and Kathleen Spencer along with many cousins nieces, and nephews in addition to a host of friends.

Rev. Beasley was a dedicated Christian and faithful member of Greater Mt. Zion Holiness Church. He served in the US Army for six years and diligently worked for M. K. Bowen Construction, Radford Arsenal, and manager of Hill's (Department Store's over shoes) for some nineteen years. He was a very loving and devoted husband, father, and grandfather as well as a servant to his community. Rev. Beasley played a key role in establishing community activities during his time as coordinator for the Christiansburg Community Center, petitioned to create sidewalks in his neighborhood, along with being an active member of the local Ruritan Club.

His family will be receiving friends at Schaeffer Memorial Baptist Church on High Street on Wednesday, January 24 from 7:00 to 9:00pm. Funeral services will be held on Thursday, January 25 at

2:00pm also at Schaeffer Memorial Baptist Church with Elder Larry Carter presiding. Arrangements by Penn's Funeral Home, 248 Randolph Ave., Pulaski, VA.

MY FATHER

My father is not perfect, in a way he's just like me,
He made mistakes and came in late, and sometimes paid a fee.
We did not always agree on the things that we did,
Thanks to you about others I do care.
Thanks to you I didn't come in late.
I didn't do some of the things that other kids would do,
That's because I knew better, after all I had to answer to you.
Now you know we have not always seen eye to eye,
But from you I learn respect and that is not a lie.
Now that you have found God you are all a father will be,
You got that special touch all others can see.
You gave me the gift of poetry so I could express the way I feel,
So I would not go through life pretending my Love's real.
On this father's day, I want you to know no matter what we've
been through,
There is no obstacle that has stopped my love for you.

Your Daughter Connie Beasley (Teele)

MOTHER'S HARD TIME

Mother, Oh Mother, I bow my head,
Thinking of the sorrow that you have shed.
When I was young I never knew,
Just how much you went through.
Now I'm old and I know,
Let me tell you how it shows.
When snow was yea so deep,
You went to work to get us food to eat.
Even when you were hungry yourself,
There was always food for us upon the shelf.
You tried hard in every way,
To keep us fed day by day.
You worked and toiled no matter what people said,
Until you were sick inside your bed.
You done for us all you could,
And treated her children like a mother should.
Now that we are grown; what can you say you gained?
A life of misery, heartache's and pain
For you, I bow my head to pray
For God to keep you day by day

S.A. Beasley Jr.
For Mama Bea

A NEGRO'S FORGOTTEN LOVE

I love you baby, with your rosy cheeks and hair so red,
But rather than see us together, some Americans would
rather see us dead.
Yet they talk a bunch of crap about Democracy
But here in America as my wife
There be no home for you and me
When they see us together they will make fun
They may let you slide baby
But they would see me hung
They can't believe there's love for people of a different race
Although we love each other baby in America some
places love does not rate
All the people would start whispering and us they would shun
Because they fail to realize we too are human

S. A. Beasley Jr. (1950)

BLACK POWER

You heard of Black Power
But it's not what it seems
I like to take this time to tell you what it means
It means the power to legislate
To help make the laws
To make sure it's doing its thing
And living up to it's cause
The power to hold the same job
Like the whites always had
To be looked upon as good
And not the one that's bad
The power to stop and eat when and where I please
And to stop at any motel lie down and sleep with ease
To be treated like a citizen, because we are human too
And we are part of the United States, born under the Red,
White and Blue
To learn to love my brother
No matter what his race might be
Be proud that I'm born black
And part of a great country
Black Power will not only help blacks
But it will help whites too
Because it will help you understand
That I'm just as great as you
We must use it with honesty
And not something to hide behind
Then Black Power will have proved its meaning?
And benefit all mankind

S. A. Beasley Jr.

THE POLITICIAN

The reptile you call a snake that crawls upon the earth
And beneath breathes dust through his nostrils
And makes his meals out of dust
No, he didn't always crawl upon the earth he was an angel
At the beginning of his birth
His face was beautiful .
Yet his heart was filled with sin
That's why he crawls upon his belly and he will until the end.

S.A. Beasley Jr.

MARRIAGE HIGHWAY

Wait, I would like to speak to you
For a moment if I may
Before you take your journey,
Down this marriage highway
There are a few things about this road that I would like
for you to know
You see I started on this road a long time ago.
The entrance if this highway is all you dreamed it to be,
And things are so beautiful as far as you can see.
But after you traveled a few miles, you find
some places mighty, rough.
And some of the mountains that you climb you'll
find them really tough.
There will be some sunshine and there will be lots of rain,
Then you realize that some parts of the road are not the same
But no matter how rough the road may get,
Or what the people might say,
Just remember the vows you made to God and you'll
make it all the way.

S.A. Beasley Jr.

BEAUTY

Have you ever taken the time from your work or play?
To gaze upon the beauty that you find each day
The singing of the birds
The humming of the bees,
The color of the grass,
The leaves upon a tree
The blue in the sky
The mountains and the sea,
The rays of the sun reflecting on its beauty
The beauty a woman possesses in a day
Do you see the beauty before they pass away?

S.A. Beasley Jr.

WHO AM I

Who am I to put to shame or to disgrace?
Regardless of his religion
Creed, Color or Race.
Who am I to tell man, the places he should or should not go?
Who am I to judge one man by the seeds that he sows?
Who am I to point the finger and condemn one man to die?
When life was given to man from the Almighty One up high
Who am I to take the right of freedom from a man?
Or down the things he believes or the platform that he stands
It was the Lord that made the earth, the people, and the stars in
the sky
And He makes the rules on earth now tell me
Who Am I

By S. A. Beasley Jr.

THE GENTLEMAN

Remember the guy who gave you candy when
you were on a date
And always apologized with courtesy whenever he was late
And even brought a flower that he gathered along the way
And father never had to speak because he never stayed to late
He would always hold your hand and open the door of the car
Brush the seat off for you to sit to watch a falling star
Where are the gentlemen?
Are there anymore?
Of all the men around there's bound to be one I'm sure
Watch out, Sadie Mae you better look around,
The guy that's knocking at your door will run you
in the ground.
They are the lovers oh No, They are in a fuss
That's no gentlemen just listen to him cuss
Look at the couple over there she's getting ready to sit
Well he didn't even hold her chair
Wait she's getting up to take off her coat
And look at him just sitting there getting ready to light a smoke
Oh there's another couple he even has a chaperone
But he's still not a gentleman he 's dancing with his hat on.
Come on Sadie Mae you can plainly see
They just don't make men like there used to be

S.A. Beasley Jr.

THE INVISIBLE EYE

There is a man at every corner a woman at the blink of the eye
Waiting and hoping that we would cheat or lie
The flirting makes us feel special we think it makes us cool
What harm would be done, if nobody ever knew
We would be back before they know no one will see a thing
It's all in fun and games what heartache could it bring?
Someone's watching what do you mean? It just could not be so,
Oh God how could I forget you go wherever I go?
Is this what I want you to see?
Is this a part of me?
Is it worth the pleasure?
Is it worth the fee . . . ?
Connie Beasley Teele

THE LETTER

Dear Friend

How are you? I just had to send a note to tell you how much I care about you. I saw you yesterday and you were talking to a friend. I waited all day hoping you would talk to me too. I gave you a sunset to close your light, and a cool breeze to rest your eyes. I waited but I still love you because you are my friend.

I saw you sleeping last night, and I longed to touch your heart so I spilled moonlight in your face, again I waited, wanting to rush down and talk.

I have so many gifts for you but you awoke and rushed off to work. My tears were in the rain that poured down upon you,If you would only listen to me you would know, I love you. I tried to tell you in the blue skies and in the quiet grass, I whispered it in the leaves and on the trees I breathed in it the color of the flowers, shouted it out in the mountain streams. Gave the birds love songs to sing. I clothed you with warm sunshine and perfume the air with nature scents, my love for you is deeper than the ocean and bigger than the biggest bleed in your heart.

Ask me Talk to me, Please don't forget me. I have so much to share with you I won't hassle you any further. It is your life now I have cherished you and I will wait . . .

Your friend Jesus

S.A. Beasley Jr.

THE MAN

Let me live in the house beside the road
And be a friend to man . . .
A lot of people here read this poem,
But few took the task at hand.
You think all these people were just a myth.
But there was such a man.
He built his house beside the road down the mountains along
the way.
No matter what your race, creed, or color
He'd give you a place to stay
He would always try to help you
Whenever he was able,
And there was always a place for you at his kitchen table
He had the greatest treasure Love
And in his heart it did not dwell,
You could measure his love and its value; we had no way to tell.
He was the world's greatest to me. One of the best friends I ever
had
I had a lot of love for him that's why we called him Dad . . . .
Everybody knew of his kindness no matter where you may go,
His name was Joseph Smith, but was known as Smoky Joe . . .

S.A. Beasley Jr.

YOUR TRUE FRIEND
NEVER LEFT

Every now and then life is tough and nothing seems to
make you smile,
You search for answers to make your day worthwhile.
Although you laugh a little, in the end your day still seems
sad and blue,
You take a nice long bath and maybe a glass of wine or two.
Yet with millions of people in the world it seems like only you.
To hold my hand and say I love you and
everything will work out,
Would keep your heart from wondering and
relieve a little doubt.
After many tears and self-pity, suddenly, you realize,
Someone has been there all the time as you look up to the sky.
He will dry all your tears and tell you it's okay,
He will stick right by your side to get you through another day,
Life does not always work by what we do or what we say,
But life will work if we just take time to pray.

A MERE MIRROR

In the hard confines of Detroit, whether working at the health club, hospital, or in a large administrative building, it was a struggle to survive. Drugs, alcohol, sex, and violence seemed to be a number one priority. Even smoking was something started at a young age, although most do not consider it a drug. Have you ever smoked and tried to stop? Cocaine can be described, as the Lays potato chip of Detroit after just one try—you can't have just one. It seems to be something you had to have, whether you were at home or at work. It consumes everything, your lifestyle, bills—even food was meaningless. When I had to choose between any one of these, cocaine won. Soon the only thing that meant anything was, Me, Myself and I. Never caring or refusing to notice that I hurt others. If it ever dared to bother me or enter my mind, I just got higher and higher until the thoughts went away.

I know some of you are thinking that all I had to do is quit. Well, put yourself in my shoes. Try to go without something that you seem to have every day, maybe just a soda or anything? A friend of mine, made a commitment to refrain from something for her class project at Howard University, she chose drinking soda. In the end she had broken her commitment eight times before quitting, and that was just for soda.

Going to my grandmas in a little country, town, called Holstein. That seems to be the only time I could get away from the chaos. Once or twice a year, I would travel to Holstein, to take care of chores that my grandma no longer could do alone. She never said it, but she knew what I needed. She constantly kept me busy when free time seemed to come my way; she would quickly remedy it by giving me more chores or errands to run.

One day in Detroit I received the news that my grandmother

had passed. My stomach balled up into knots. I wanted so much for her to see me straight. As I sat in the confines of my room, suddenly realizing I had everything, yet nothing. As a child my father took me on a visit to the prison, the men inside were yelling at me, as if I was some kind of sex object they could not wait to put their hands on. I never forgot how my body started shivering and shaking. Even then I vowed my life would not end in prison.

The mirror in the corner of the room seemed to stand out, calling me to come. To dare take a look, inside at my own reflection. I hesitated only briefly; suddenly felt challenged. I accepted the challenge, not wanting a mere mirror to gain victory over me. For the first time in five years I saw my sunken face, my thieving hands, me an addict . . . on the verge of being caught up in a life of crime and violence. In my mind once again were the men in the prison calling me their "lady". I fell to my knees, and cried, like a newborn child. Oh, mirror, oh mirror look at me what have I become?

I started praying to what I then thought was somebody. I did not know to whom I was praying, but I wanted someone to hear my cry. Before I knew it, the signs of daybreak were coming through the window shades. Again I was faced with another day on the streets of Detroit. As I walked out the door it seemed to be the first time ever I noticed the blue skies and the sun creeping over the land. The sun seemed to be sneaking a peak at my life, as if to see if my life had changed. My 'dawg' approached the crib with the usual supply of drugs. In my heart I was saying no, in my mind I screamed, "I need__." Money seems to be shorter and shorter and I never seem to have enough. I found myself going into to the house finding something to bargain with and bargain I did. The only problem, it was Moms house, and things. My heart said no, my body, screaming, "I need"

I hustled, finding a place to go and fulfill my bodies need. I noticed the sun seemed to pull up a little higher than before. As if to get a better view of me." "What are you looking at" I said. "I will quit don't worry, I will quit." Suddenly a little boy approaches and just stops in his tracks and looks at me saying "Mister what, are you doing?" I did not want the young boy to see what I was doing so I hid my drugs and tried to blow him off. But the persistent brat, kept pulling my pants leg, saying "Mister what you doing?" My neighbor came out onto her porch and sat in her swing slowly rocking. Her face had changed, suddenly, it was no longer my neighbor's face but the face of my grandmother, the grandmother I wanted to show that I could be somebody. I fell on my knees and cried. I ran like a sprinter into the house and rapidly put a few items in a bag. Next thing I knew, I was boarding a bus to Holstein. I did not know what I was going to do once I arrived, but I knew I could go to my grandma's house so at least I would have a roof over my head. I remembered when I use to come to Holstein and visit, I met a few people but one stayed in my mind. There was something about her, maybe it's because she was a country girl, maybe it's because she seemed to appreciate all the things I said and the activities I used to be able to do. I was a decent athlete in my day. If I get myself together, I think Shanika and I can have a lot of fun together. The thought that continued to enter my mind was to call her. However picking up the phone was the last thing on my mind, lying down was the first. For some reason, today, I feel more tired than ever before. My body seemed to shiver. I was cold, then hot; I craved the cocaine from the city.

This time, Grandma will be proud of me. So for weeks that seemed like years I toughen it out—help was coming from somewhere deep inside of me. I knew that I had to survive. The road would not be easy. Even small towns carried the same problems of drugs, alcohol, sex, and violence. Focusing was the key to overcoming my addiction and defeating the challenge in which I now embarked. I contemplated, "Where do I go from here?"

My mom when she visited my grandmother always left behind a supply of books. I found myself lonely and thought that maybe one book would help ease the emptiness that now laid deep inside. The book was called "Too Late." The story tells of a person with everything, yet nothing, he is a millionaire who had four or five women and a wife. There were people always trying to speak to him about God; he would just laugh. One day the whole world seemed to change right in front of his eyes. Upon returning from a trip, he stood in an overly crowded airport and turned his head for only a second. When he looked back people were missing, the same ones that were always preaching the gospel. Everyone else seemed to be still around. At first, he thought it was a quick retreat on their part (to get out of the airport) but as he went outside cars were lined up. The cars were traveling and crashing into each other with no one behind the wheel. As I continued to read the man occasionally saw a driver or two. The drivers were frightened and speechless as if they too had seen a ghost. The book got me thinking about the end of time, fear seemed to come over me.

The ring of the telephone made me jump, I immediately answered. It was Shanika, the one that had remained in my thoughts. What do I say? Am I ready to see others? "Slow down," my heart said, and for once my mind agreed. Conversation after conversation helped each day get easier. Finally, I could see light and the light was the woman that constantly stayed deep inside my soul from the moment we met—I never understood why. Upon finally, getting together face-to-face I felt different. My energy was anew. My challenges and goals became larger. Shanika spoke on my thoughts of the supernatural, hers of God. Soon we agreed, that God is real, and yes, God is super natural.

When I returned home, I quickly picked up the book, "Too Late," to finish my reading with anticipation and curiosity. The man went back home, to all of his women and continued to party, not seeming to have any concern for the events he had witnessed. Suddenly boom a great ball of fire fell on the building and they all started burning feeling every cringe, and crying out for help. Seven days and seven nights you could hear cries out into the world. The book ended and the author announced the next book, which was the sequel. "No thanks," I said to myself, "I have had enough." The thought of the book ran over and over in my head. It reminded me of how I didn't care about anything that was happening around me. That was part of my life that will never be forgotten or repeated. I soon became thankful for the obstacles that I had faced, realizing that human instinct sometimes will try to play tricks on your realities.

Shanika and I started going to church. We learned that even small things could not be done without God. I automatically began praying constantly. Every now and then I think about doing something but since I started praying it was kind of weird, it seemed as if something would intervene. Something as simple, like a phone call, or something as large as a thunderstorm. Soon my world started changing, new job, new energy, and a new body and a feeling deep down inside of inner peace. All these years, I thought, being in church was a boring life, no more friends, no more cookouts, and no more laughs. I have more fun than ever, laughing, working out, and sharing the gospel. I consider everyone my friend. Funny I kept searching for that inner peace in drugs. It was there all along. I was just searching in the wrong place. Life with God was inexpensive, and my soul felt the high it was always trying to get. I 'm not defeated with God's help my life is now complete.

The sun seems to shine high and full and the gleam is now warm, not judging. I ran to the challenging, daring mirror and the reflection of a muscular, healthful new body is what I saw. The power and glory of our Lord and Savior provided me with Shanika, the same woman that I carried in my soul for years. Together we now have become evenly yoked with the grace of God. Shanika had stood by me when I was down. Now we will stand by each other we shall till death, do us part. What I enjoy now is being a testimony and converting souls to God. Sure, deep inside my mind, the thought of drugs, remain, but now it's my soul that wins not the devil. The challenges are there, but the choices are also. The fellows still try to get me to hang out and once I went. You know I wasn't happy; I felt the cold reality of the real world, all about self. It was no longer what made me feel complete. Shanika, love for God, and life's changes help me provide the inner peace my body longed for. No one will change that. I don't want my life without God. Hey, who said it was going to be easy, challenges are a good thing it is what helps me stay on my toes always fighting for the upper hand.

I feel like my grandma is resting peacefully. I think back to how my grandmother used to tell me the things she and my ancestors endured, slavery, being raped just to name a few. Even Mom had to go through not eating at the same restaurants or drinking from the same water fountains as whites. Their life was harder than we could ever imagine. The blood that runs within their veins is the same blood running today through ours. And if I can remember correctly it was God and good ole gospel songs that kept their spirits up. You and I could only wonder, why, I did not think of that a long time ago. The new age can be spoiling, but we cannot, and must not Let go of the strong roots we have inherited. Thanks to God, we can and shall overcome. A lot of things go on in life and no one said that it was going to be easy. Now I realize that it's not about what happens, it's about how we chose to handle what happens. Just because statistics says it's so does not mean we have to make it so. If I can make a change, so can anyone.

My mom was so proud, I handed her an envelope of money. I found the prefect card letting her know that I realize that heartbreak could not be bought, but maybe some of the materials could be replaced. I wanted her to come and live with my wife and me and she was overjoyed. The comfort of mom seeing daily how my life had changed was if Grandma was still here. I do not go a single day without going outside looking for the sun only wishing we could give each other a high five. Mirrors are no longer in the corner of the room in our house; the hallway walls are designed with mirrors as a constant reminder of the challenging mirror. My job has sent me to college and I have almost completed my masters. Shanika is still by my side as my wife, and in another month we will have little Sergio Stevens, Jr., Another challenge then begins.

Constance Beasley Teele